Frogs and Crayons

A Day in the Life of Any School

by

Geoffrey May

Frogs and Crayons: A Day in the Life of Any School

Copyright © by Geoffrey May
First Edition 2025

Road to Awesome, LLC.

ROAD TO AWESOME

To my dad and uncles –
who taught me how to listen
and tell a good story.

My goal for this book is not to make fun of anyone or anything. I just want to remind you that, as teachers, we have a hard job. There are days when nothing is funny or seems to have a purpose or place. You get to be the bird, or you get to be the statue. You have to remember to laugh when it gets hard. If you don't, you are going to have a very tough time keeping your sanity.

Every morning I pick a student I work with to help put the flags up. They enjoy the job, the sense of prestige, and most importantly, the positive attention.

One morning, we found that a tree frog had moved into the box covering the flag rope. I decided, as any good teacher would, to show the frog to my assistant along with the other kids who had gathered. When I reached for the frog, it decided I was a threat and jumped to flee from danger.

As it leaped from my attempted teachable moment, it did what frogs do in a threatening situation and let out a stream of pee to defend itself. My flag helper found himself in the line of fire as the frog flew over his head with no more than a quarter of an inch to spare. He caught the brunt of the defensive line in his face.

Thankfully, we were masked up due to the COVID pandemic. I lost it and began to laugh uncontrollably. I got him to the nurse quickly. He was grumbling that I better not tell anyone, but he slowly found it funny.

What came next was a very awkward phone call to his mom. I explained what had happened, and she replied with, "Good. He was giving me a rough time this morning!"

Kind of like a doctor, I do rounds to check on my kids in their classrooms. A first grader had recently been added to my roster. I checked on him in his homeroom and found him with a green crayon in one nostril and a pink crayon in the other. He was looking around the room, seemingly, contemplating the meaning of life.

I came in and put my hand on his shoulder and said, "Dude, what are you doing? Do you need some help?" The crayons blew out and clattered to the desk. He answered with all the wisdom of a first grader, "Nothing..."

Actual Kid Quote

"I am having a good day because I put my good boy pants on."

Some of the students I work with have behavior problems, and some days, I spend a lot of time dealing with tantrums. After a two-hour screaming session, I needed a break. So, I decided to walk the halls a bit and clear my head.

As I came around the corner into the third grade hallway, I found two of my kids by the rest room in full meltdown mode due to their issues from being on the autism spectrum.

One was screaming and crying, "I do not want to be a girl!! I don't want to go to the girl's room!!! Barack Obama is going to make me be a transsexual!!!" The other one was flapping his arms, pacing and screaming, "I was just a little bit naked. I was just a little bit naked. My mama is going to kill me..." over and over.

To make this storm even more fun, other students were coming back in from recess. Their teacher, who was kind of crusty anyway, wanted me to write a referral for these students and call administration. So much for my break.

I calmed the teacher down and sent the kids to my room. Come to find out, it was a very special education moment. One student had walked into the bathroom and seen the other student's back side because his pants were pulled down too far at the urinal. The other one was watching too much news in the morning before he came to school.

So, I told one to make sure his pants were pulled up because no one wanted to see his butt. To the other, I said, "No one wants to have their bathroom business shared."

I sent them back to class and moved on. I never got my break that day, but sometimes, that is the way it goes.

At one point in my career, I worked with a student who had a very hard life and a long history of violent behaviors. One day, when he was in an escalated state and approaching full crisis, I called for backup from the counselor and administration.

He threw every insult at us he could think of. We were given directions on where we could go, how we could get there and what to do when we arrived. He looked at the assistant principal and said, "Your ass is so big, it is like a tube of Pillsbury dough biscuits that exploded..."

Without missing a beat, she looked at me and said, "Do I have a big, biscuit ass?" The kid shut his mouth, and well, I did not have anything to say either.

Actual Kid Quote

"I have muddy undies.
Can I go the nurse?"

*(He really did fall in the mud, but
it was worth the trip to the nurse
to see her expression.)*

Many years ago, the state of Texas mandated that students needed to practice bus safety annually. The Transportation Department would send over a group of busses and line them up. The drivers would coach the kids on what to do in the event of an accident. The kids would practice evacuating through the back door, then everyone would go back inside the school.

The bus I was helping with ran into trouble right away. The driver and monitor had almost no control. The back of the bus was like watching monkeys at a zoo. Well, I decided the only way I could reel them in was to bang on the window.

I banged on the window once, nothing. Then, I banged again, nothing. The third time was the charm. The window cracked and shattered. A domino like wave of kids sitting down went through the bus, and the kids got quiet. I panicked and headed straight to my principal's office. I told him what had happened and said I would pay for the window. He asked me, "Well, did they get quiet?" When I affirmed that they had indeed gotten quiet, he half smiled, then told me, "Don't worry about it…"

Many years later, while getting an oil change, the shop manager kept looking at me like he knew me. When he finally remembered who I was, he said, "Do you remember the time we were out of control on the bus and you punched out the window? "

Swear words do not have a place in everyday conversation, especially in schools. However, I have been known to repeat a word or two a student is using to take the power away from them.

For example:

Student- "You are a motherfucker..."

Me-"That is right. I am Mr. Motherfucker, and I deserve some respect please because I am in charge..."

The kid looked dumbfounded and stopped cussing. No power, no point in saying bad words.

Actual Kid Quote

"Is that an inside smell?"

While on breakfast duty one morning, I saw a first grader wearing a Batman T-shirt. Feeling a bit mischievous, I asked him if he talked different when wore that shirt.

He looked down and said in a much deeper, booming voice, "Yes."

This kid is going places!

Actual Kid Quote

"My teacher is kindly oppressed with me. She said I did amazing, great work. I didn't go to the office, and I stayed awake!!"

One day, one of my students asked to go the bathroom. When he was gone a long time, I got worried.

I approached the bathroom and heard giggling followed by a thud. I opened the door to catch him showing a group of kindergarteners how to use the hand dryer like a cannon. They were squeezing wet paper towels out, wading them up, stuffing them in the blower, and then shooting them at the ceiling. I knew I had to get onto him a bit, but I have to admit I was very impressed with the level of thought it took to accomplish that.

On occasion, I get text messages from teachers requesting that I deal with my student's problem behaviors.

Text message from another teacher- "Hey, he is stuck on the monkey bars."

My text back- "Ok, on the way."

I head to the playground not knowing what to expect.

Text message from the teacher- "It's ok; he fell."

Actual Kid Quote

"What does my hand smell like?"

There is nothing like having to settle first graders down during a lock down drill with a substitute teacher. Nothing like getting a text from another teacher letting you know you have a student in the bathroom during a lockdown drill. Nothing like having to explain to the principals and the security consultant that you have a kid in the bathroom. Nothing like getting asked every two minutes, "Can I flush yet?" Nothing like having to say, "No." Nothing like having to wait for the all clear and then getting him back to class. Nothing like not being able to avoid the bad jokes that followed…

A first grader stands up and announces to his table group that he has tooted. Then, each student in his group proceeds to smell his chair for residual odors.

We are doomed.

Actual Kid Quote

"Why is there a string on my wiener?"

A student of mine, who was taking a break in the motor lab on the swing, started asking me questions about animal noises. She would swing back and forth a bit, then ask things like, "What does a duck say?" or "What does a cow say?" This went on and on.

Finally, she got a puzzled look and said, "What does a shark say?" This threw me off a bit, so I asked back, "I don't know, what does the shark say?" She thought a minute and then responded with "Do, Doo, Do, Doo...."

(For those that don't know, she was singing the Baby Shark song.)

One of my behavior kids was not settling down. He demanded to see the principal because he felt he was being bullied. We head to the office and interrupt the principal, who was busy. The kid proceeds to go into a rant about chicken choking while in the bathroom. (Ask a friend if you do not know).

He was in no way choking his chicken in the bathroom. The principal sent the kid into the hall and asked me what in the world he was talking about with the chicken choking. After explaining it, he handed us off to the behavior counselor.

After the student left, the counselor took a plastic bead necklace and tied it around the neck of a rubber chicken. She hung the chicken on the back of the student's desk. It stayed there for at least a week.

Actual Kid Quote

"What do you smell like?"

Sight words can tell you a lot about how a student is engaging in the work you are doing with them. Sometimes, this happens in very interesting ways.

A teacher told me she had a student read the word country. After reading and sounding out the word country, he said, "I am country."

He then told a story about his grandmother and squirrel season. He explained how they hunted squirrel on her property. Then he said, "You know you can eat squirrel? How do you like squirrel when you eat it? Well, you can have squirrel hot dogs, hamburgers, fried squirrel..." He very quickly started sounding like a red neck version of Bubba's shrimp speech in *Forrest Gump*.

I'm not sure if they ever got back to the lesson.

Actual Kid Quote

"They said the A word…."

"They said the B word…."

"They said the F word…."

"They said the S word…."

"They said the V word…."

(That last one I could never figure out. Some days there is not enough Tylenol to fix it all.)

"Hey, on your way out of the cafeteria, could you tell the boys to quit trying to lick their armpits?"

As I said earlier, we may be doomed.

Actual Kid Quote

"You better look out if I have a #9
from Chick-fil-A..."

After a rough day, one of my behavior kids assured me that he was only going to have one bag of Taki's for his snack today. I asked why. That was where I made my mistake. If you ask a question, you have to be ready for the answer. His response was, "I am only having one bag today so I do not pass out in the bathroom." I had to ask...

Actual Kid Quote

"We don't say the F word
around granny…"
(From a Pre-K student
walking to the bus)

Acknowledgements

I would like to thank all the teachers and people, both in and out of school, that helped keep me moving forward.

About the Author

Walmart Department Manager to Special Education teacher was a very long, strange trip. Geoffrey kept thinking he would figure out what it was he wanted to do. Even with his parents both being teachers, he never intended to become an educator. He is not sure where or when he began to realize that teaching was what he needed to do, but Geoffrey ended up graduating from McMurry University in Abilene, Texas in 1991.

After 26 years, he now thinks he might know a thing or two. On the other hand, he feels maybe it's best that he keep himself convinced otherwise.

More Books from Road to Awesome

Taking the Leap: A Field Guide for Aspiring
School Leaders by Robert F. Breyer

Transform: Techy Notes to Make Learning
Sticky by Debbie Tannenbaum

Becoming Principal: A Leadership Journey &
The Story of School Community
by Dr. Jeff Prickett

Elevate Your Vibe: Action Planning with
Purpose by Lisa Toebben

#OwnYourEpic: Leadership Lessons in Owning
Your Voice and Your Story by Dr. Jay Dostal

The Design Thinking, Entrepreneurial,
Visionary Planning Leader:
A Practical Guide for Thriving in Ambiguity
by Dr. Michael Nagler

Becoming the Change: Five Essential
Elements to Being Your Best Self by Dan Wolfe

inspired: moments that matter
by Melissa Wright

Foundations of Instructional Coaching: Impact
People, Improve Instruction, Increase Success
by Ashley Hubner

Out of the Trenches: Stories of Resilient
Educators by Dana Goodier

Principled Leader
by Bobby Pollicino

Road to Awesome: The Journey of a Leader
by Darrin Peppard

When Calling Parents Isn't Your Calling: A
teacher's guide to communicating with all
parents by Crystal Frommert

Struggle to Strength: Finding the Ingredients
to Your Secret Sauce by Kip Shubert

Guiding Transformational Change in
Education by Kristina V. Mattis

Be the Cause: An Educator's Guide to
EFFECTive Instruction by Josh Korb

Called to Empower
by Coach Kurt Hines

The Blueprint: Survive and Thrive as a School
Administrator
by Todd M. Bloomer

Sustaining Excellence: How Culture Drives
Teacher Retention
by Martin Silverman

Kid's Books from
Road to Awesome

Road to Awesome A Journey for Kids
by Jillian DuBois and Darrin M. Peppard

Emersyn Blake and the Spotted Salamander
by Kim Collazo

Theodore Edward Makes a New Friend
by Alyssa Schmidt

I'm Autistic and I'm Awesome
by Derek Danziger

Emersyn Blake and the Stalked Jellyfish
by Kim Collazo

Birdie & Mipps
by Barbara Gruener

Teddy the Tiny Tree
by Derek Danziger

roadtoawesome.net/books